D1537631

*For Conor and Aidan*

# A Color and Learn Book

# The Story of van Gogh And Gauguin

## Lisa Alexandra Frey

**Starshell Press**

All rights reserved. No part of this publication may be reproduced or transmitted in any form or by any means electronic or mechanical, including photocopying, recording, or any information storage and retrieval system, without permission from the publisher

Copyright 2001 Starshell Press
Quogue, New York
Reprinted 2002

ISBN 09707110-0-X


Published by: Starshell Press
Lisa A Frey, Publisher
Designed  by Jane Darroch Riley
Illustrated by Scott Riley
Produced by Reliance Production Company Ltd
Printed and bound in China

**Front Cover Paintings:**
Vincent van Gogh:Self -Portrait with Fur Cap, Bandaged Ear and Pipe AKG Berlin / Superstock
Paul Gauguin: Self- Portrait In Caricature, National Gallery, London / Superstock
**Back Cover Paintings:**
Paul Gauguin:Two Women of Tahiti, Staatliche Kunstsammlungen Dresden
Gemaldegalerie Neue Meister, Dresden,
Vincent van Gogh:Vincent's Bedroom in Arles,Amsterdam, Van Gogh Museum
(Vincent van Gogh Foundation)
Paul Gauguin:Old Women at Arles, Mr and Mrs Lewis Larned Coburn Memorial Collection,
1934, photograph, The Art Institute of Chicago
Vincent van Gogh:Boats at Les Saintes-Maries,Reindert Groot, Fotografie, Amsterdam

Read about the friendship between these two famous artists. Look closely at how they use color in their paintings. Use the outlines to create your own masterpieces.

Vincent van Gogh was born in Holland in 1853.

Paul Gauguin was born in France in 1848.

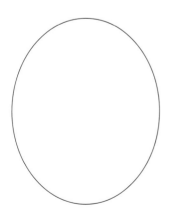

I was born in  _____

My birthday is  _____

Draw your face or paste in your photo

Paul Gauguin
Self-Portrait, with portrait of Emile Bernard, Les Miserables
Amsterdam, Van Gogh Museum (Vincent van Gogh Foundation)

A little more than 100 years ago, in a town in northern France, there lived a painter called Paul Gauguin. He painted this picture of himself, and sent it to the painter Vincent van Gogh. He signed the painting, "to my friend, Vincent."

Can you see Vincent's name on the painting?

Vincent van Gogh
Self-Portrait
Fogg Art Museum
Cambridge, Massachusetts/Superstock

Van Gogh was excited to see his friend's painting. He had also just finished his self-portrait, which he said made him look Japanese. He sent it to Gauguin. The writing on the painting, *"to my friend, Paul Gauguin,"* has faded away over the years.

Vincent van Gogh
Boats at Les Saintes-Maries
Reindert Groot, Fotografie, Amsterdam

Van Gogh lived in Arles, a town in southern France. He liked painting outside near his home. Here is his painting of boats resting on the shore. One of the boats is named "Amitie" which is French for "friendship."

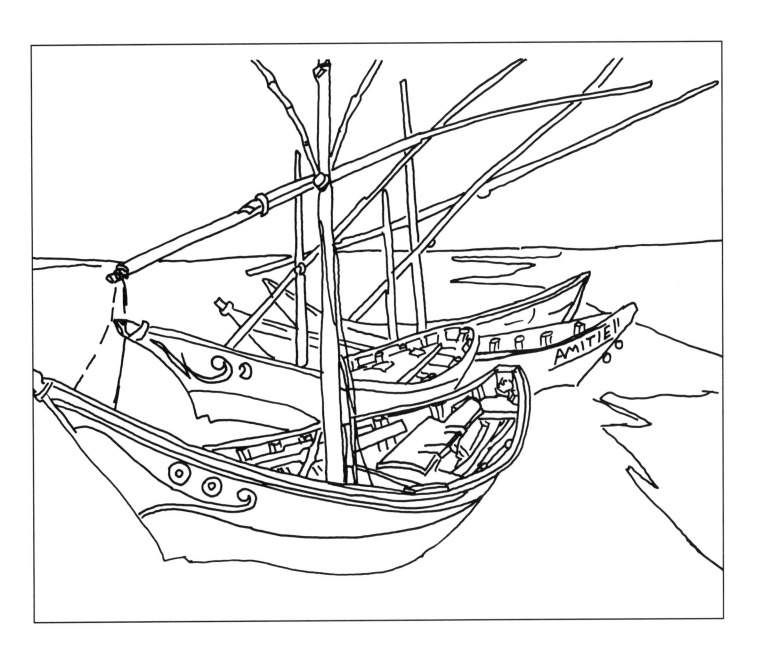

Can you see the name of the boat?
Choose a name for the boat with the yellow mast and
write it on your drawing.

Paul Gauguin
The Vision After the Sermon, Jacob Wrestling an Angel
National Gallery of Scotland/Superstock

Meanwhile in northern France, Gauguin created one of his most famous paintings ever. In it, a man called Jacob wrestles an angel with yellow wings. Local women in white hats pray with a priest.

If you look closely you can see a cow about to join the fight.

Which person is the priest?

How many others are watching?

Vincent van Gogh
Vincent's Bedroom in Arles
Amsterdam, Van Gogh Museum (Vincent van Gogh Foundation)

One summer, van Gogh invited Gauguin to his home in Arles so that they could paint together. Van Gogh painted this picture of his bedroom just before Gauguin arrived.

You can see an extra chair in the room for Gauguin. Look for a hat, a bearded face, a tree, a mirror, a pitcher, a glass, six window panes and a towel with a red stripe.

Paul Gauguin
Night Cafe at Arles
Museum of Modern Western Art, Moscow
Bridgeman Art Library, London/SuperStock

Gauguin arrived in Arles very early in the morning. It was too early to knock on Vincent's door, so Gauguin went to the cafe by the train station. The owner, Madame Ginoux, knew van Gogh well and recognized Gauguin from his self-portrait. During his stay with van Gogh, Gauguin returned to paint Madame Ginoux in her cafe. She sits at a table with an old-fashioned soda bottle.

Look for: Madame Ginoux's cat, 9 polka dots, a netted hat, two biscuits, 3 balls, smoke in the air and Gauguin's name.

Write your name in your own style here:

_____

Vincent van Gogh
Night Cafe in Arles
AKG Photo, Berlin

Madame Ginoux's cafe was van Gogh's favorite meeting place. He liked to go there late at night. In his painting of the cafe, a couple of men are asleep at their tables.

What time does the clock say?
Look at the table tops, the pool table and the walls, then look back at Gauguin's painting of Madame Ginoux. How many things are the same in the two paintings?
Can you find Madame Ginoux's soda bottle?

Paul Gauguin
Portrait of van Gogh Painting Sunflowers
Amsterdam, Van Gogh Museum (Vincent van Gogh Foundation)

Gauguin and van Gogh liked to paint together outdoors in the afternoon. One day while van Gogh was painting sunflowers, Gauguin painted his friend at work.

Look at the paints on the palette van Gogh is holding.
How many of the colors on the palette can you find in the painting?
Can you find all five sunflowers?

Vincent van Gogh
The Painter on the Road to Tarascon
Amsterdam, Van Gogh Museum (Vincent van Gogh Foundation)

Van Gogh also painted himself outside. In this painting he carries his paints and brushes on his back, on the way to paint another outdoor scene. The long stick he holds is his fold-up easel.

Look at the trees and the ground. What season do you think it is?
Look at the painter's shadow. Where do you think the sun is?

Paul Gauguin
Old Women at Arles
Mr. and Mrs. Lewis Larned Coburn Memorial Collection
The Art Institute of Chicago

Here is Gauguin's picture of the garden across from van Gogh's house. Some say if you look hard enough you can see the painter's face in the green bush. Others say the woman in the front is Madame Ginoux.

What do you think?
Can you draw your own face in
the green bush?

Vincent van Gogh
Self-Portrait with Fur Cap, Bandaged Ear and Pipe
AKG Berlin /Superstock

Unfortunately Gauguin and van Gogh fought during this visit. After two months, Gauguin left. Van Gogh was very upset. He painted himself with a bandage on the side of his face where he cut his ear.

You can see the smoke coming from van Gogh's pipe. In what other painting can you see pipe-smoke?

Paul Gauguin
Self- Portrait In Caricature
National Gallery, London / Superstock

Gauguin returned to the north, and he too painted a picture of himself looking sad. Even though the friends had parted, in some ways they still painted as though they were together.

Look at the background colors. What other
paintings have red and orange walls?

 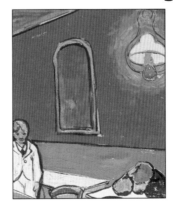 

Paul Gauguin
Two Women of Tahiti
Gemaldegalerie Neue Meister, Dresden

After he left van Gogh, Gauguin made his first trip to Tahiti, an island far from France.
He painted pictures of local women that made him famous. These paintings were popular in France, where he sent them to be sold.

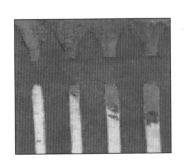  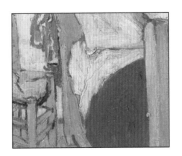 

Even though Tahiti looked very different from France, Gauguin liked to paint with the same colors. Look at the red in these pictures. Can you guess which paintings they come from?

Vincent van Gogh
Vase with Sunflowers
Amsterdam, Van Gogh Museum (Vincent van Gogh Foundation)

Van Gogh sold only one painting in his lifetime. He lived for just two years after Gauguin left. His friends brought his favorite flowers, sunflowers, to his funeral. Many years later, van Gogh became as famous as Gauguin, and this colorful picture of sunflowers is now one of the most loved in the world.

Write your name on the vase like van Gogh and
draw in your favorite flowers.
Look back at the flowers in
Gauguin's painting on page 18.
Which painting of sunflowers do
you prefer?

Paintings in this book were reproduced with permission from the following sources:

## Vincent van Gogh

Page 5:     **Self-Portrait**, Fogg Art Museum,Cambridge, Massachusetts/Superstock
Page 7:     **Self-Portrait**, Fogg Art Musem, Cambridge, Massachusetts/Superstock
Page 8:     **Boats at Les Saintes-Maries**, Reindert Groot, Fotografie, Amsterdam
Page 12:    **Vincent's Bedroom in Arles**, Amsterdam, Van Gogh Museum (Vincent van Gogh Foundation)
Page 16:    **Night Cafe in Arles**, AKG Photo, Berlin
Page 20:    **The Painter on the Road to Tarascon**, Destroyed in the Second World War; formerly Kaiser Friedrich Museum, Magdebrug, B.V.'t Lanthuys, Amsterdam, Van Gogh Museum (Vincent van Gogh Foundation)
Page 24:    **Self-Portrait with Fur Cap, Bandaged Ear and Pipe**, AKG Berlin/Superstock
Page 30:    **Vase with Sunflowers**, Amsterdam, Van Gogh Museum (Vincent van Gogh Foundation)

## Paul Gauguin

Page 5:     **Self-Portrait, with portrait of Emile Bernard, Les Miserables**, Amsterdam, Van Gogh Museum (Vincent van Gogh Foundation)
Page 6:     **Self-Portrait, with portrait of Emile Bernard, Les Miserables**, Amsterdam, Van Gogh Museum (Vincent van Gogh Foundation)
Page 10:    **The Vision After the Sermon, Jacob Wrestling an Angel**, National Gallery of Scotland/Superstock
Page 14:    **Night Cafe at Arles**, Museum of Modern Western Art, Moscow Bridgeman Art Library, London/SuperStock
Page 18:    **Portrait of van Gogh Painting Sunflowers**, Amsterdam, Van Gogh Museum (Vincent van Gogh Foundation)
Page 22:    **Old Women at Arles,** Mr. and Mrs. Lewis Larned Coburn Memorial Collection, photograph, The Art Institute of Chicago
Page 26:    **Self-Portrait In Caricature**, National Gallery, London/Superstock
Page 28:    **Two Women of Tahiti,** Staatliche Kunstsammlungen Dresden Gemaldegalerie Neue Meister, Dresden, Photo:Jurgen Karpinski